UNCAGED

RELEASE YOUR INNER QUEEN

Nyisha Tilus

Scripture quotations marked NKJV are taken from the New King James Version. Copyright © 1982 by Thomas Nelson. Used by permission. All rights reserved.

Book Design & Layout: Brooke & Lee Co.
Cover & Author Photo: Shawn Hanna
Book Editing: iPromise Media & Brooke & Lee Co.

ISBN: 979-8-71-634209-5

DEDICATION

This book is dedicated to anyone ready to step into their fullness.

In life, we have become conditioned to conform to the script of others. This script always seems to dictate whether we are good enough, worth it, or even capable. I know this because for a long time, I questioned myself. I felt like I wasn't good enough - like I wasn't worthy or even capable of anything other than what I was told. I believed every negative thing that was said about and to me. Truthfully, I didn't realize that they were all bars that eventually surrounded me and inevitably caged me in. So, when I say that this book is for you, I say that because I was once you. I'm sure that we've all had moments where we've felt caged in some way or another. Since I was once in your shoes, I can tell you with certainty that, darling, you have the keys to unlock the cage that has kept you bound. If the cage doesn't unlock, well sweetie, you also have the power to break out of it.

So, here's to not allowing anyone to keep us caged in... not even ourselves.

It's time to step into the uncaged you.

This is your UNCAGING!

FOREWORD

By: Zemi Stewart

Langston Hughes began his poem "Mother to Son" with the words of a wise mother sharing with her son that "Life for me ain't been no crystal stair." Nyisha's first work, *Uncaged: Release Your Inner Queen*, reminds me so much of that poem because Nyisha has experienced the cracks, the splinters, the scarcity, and the harshness of life, but all along, she has kept climbing to freedom. *Uncaged* is her story of becoming free and is a blueprint for so many who come after her to follow. Each chapter has "break free keys" that encourage her readers to rise above their circumstances, no matter how dark and bleak, to be free: free from low self-esteem, free from the opinions of others, free from limiting beliefs, and free from self.

Women and men of any age will enjoy reading this book. Parents will be afforded a deeper understanding of their children, and young people will know that they are not alone in their struggles and that there is life on the other side of unhappiness and hopelessness. Those of us in speaking professions - pastors, teachers, coaches, and inspirational speakers - can lift so many lessons to expound upon for our audiences. However, the intent of this book is not to view it from the lens of, "How can I use this book for others?" but "How can I use this book for myself?", "How can I break free?", "How can I be made whole?", "How can I be uncaged?"

As you journey through these pages, Nyisha will help you answer those questions by exploring the themes of her own life. We see the growth of a woman who spent so many years facing dysfunction, insecurities, bullying, abuse, poverty - - and then so many more years running from potential, from danger, from purpose to somehow stumble into a room, walk on her tippy toes and change the course of her entire life.

You will see your inner child in these pages, your mother in these pages, your friends in these pages, your children in these pages, and ultimately you will see yourself in these pages. Nyisha will encourage you to champion a cause beyond yourself, lift up your head to the rising sun, and begin an awe-inspiring walk to freedom.

CONTENTS

INTRODUCTION

I was the girl in sweatpants, and if you were looking for me, I could always be found hanging out with the boys. My tomboyish nature sometimes got the best of me, and I had no idea that I was in the process of becoming so much more.

Some people would call my journey "A tale from Rags to Riches" or even "Pit to Palace." Looking back at the path that was set before me, I realize that I've been preparing for my uncaging for some ten years now. The evolution of what would be the purest and truest form of me all started when a little tomboy did the unthinkable, the unbelievable. She entered a beauty pageant.

I can hear you now, "it's not that unbelievable!" Well, for me, it was! I wasn't interested in being a girly girl at all because I didn't consider myself "one of the girls." Honestly, they made me feel painfully out of place. I didn't wear a dress until after high school. Therefore, entering a beauty pageant, given those circumstances, along with my tomboyish nature made pageantry something that was totally out of the box for me.

I didn't dream about being in a pageant, going to prom, nor even getting married. I even questioned whether I was in the right body.

Crazy right? I know!

Interestingly, the common denominator among those scenarios was that they all drew attention to me or required me to be in the forefront.

Being in a pageant also required me to highlight or show off the beauty that I believe I lacked. Since I believed that I fell short in that area, I avoided it altogether. Me, the ugly duckling that almost everyone seemed to consider me as, until I eventually believed it as well.

I've been called so many names and been rejected so many times that I allowed the negative words spoken into my life to determine the way I viewed and valued myself. Then the game changed, and my life was never again the same.

MISPLACED TRUTH

As a child, I remember looking up to my mom and her friends. They were gorgeous! They had the perfect figures, complexions, wardrobes - you name it. I looked forward to the days they came over for their "girl talk" at our house.

Yes, yes I know. Although I wasn't one of the "girls" … duh, I felt like one of them. When I knew that they were on their way over, I would ensure that I was strategically cleaning, helping, or doing homework in the area where "girl talk" was taking place or as close to it as possible.

For as long as I could remember, I felt like they had the answers to the questions that I couldn't just come out and ask. The things they spoke about fascinated me, from stories about the men in their lives to their beauty tricks.

I'll stop you right there!

I didn't think that I was a grown woman or cared about what the men in their lives were doing; I was more intrigued with the conversations that focused on self-confidence, what to and not to wear and what to and not to do. You know, things of that nature.

Their girl talk was like data collection for me. It was like reading the hot stuff in the magazine, well, minus the reading. There were instances when girl talk expanded to girl vs. guy talk, and that was my cue to go incognito. Yet, I was still interested in getting a male perspective on what guys looked for in women. "So Nyisha, why didn't you just search the web or read a magazine to get the info?"

"Maga... who? Ha!" Who needed a magazine when I had front-row seats in real life!

There were so many missing pieces to the puzzle, so many things I needed clarity on. For me, those conversations were my way of sorting through and attaining the pieces I needed.

I was being conditioned to the idea of being a woman, which I was taught was based on being clean, knowing how to clean, cook and take care of the house.

I did spring cleaning, which took place every day: toted 5-gallon buckets and actual gallons of water to and fro and ironing clothes at my neighbor's neighbor's neighbor's house (you know what I mean). I also sat in front of a kevett (a huge plastic tub) and hand-washed the laundry for everyone in the house every Saturday, religiously. I mastered the art of cooking, cleaning, and taking care of the house. Still, by default (because it was beyond my control), I really couldn't get myself together. What's interesting is that I didn't quite have an issue with being a keeper of the home; I struggled with knowing how to pamper myself, demand attention, and walk-in confidence.

I wanted to know how to fix myself. I felt like everything that could go wrong in the making of Nyisha went wrong. I didn't think I was beautiful, I lacked confidence, and it showed. I wanted to know what I needed to do to fix my body, to fix me, and that's where girl talk came in. I wanted to fit in; I wanted to look better, feel better, and feel like I was good enough.

I always heard about my mom's amazing coca-cola body that would cause both men and even women to double-take; I for certain didn't have her slim physique. I constantly heard how I was shaped like a two by four (plywood), no front or back. I was Little Miss Straight and Narrow.

I was teased about my enormous feet, I sucked my bottom lip, which caused a dark ring to form around my lips, and it didn't stop there. I had bat ears, a sharp but wide nose, and I was reminded daily of my offensive body odor.

But hey, at least at some point, I started to develop things called breasts that were just growing out of control if you asked me, but at least it made me a girl. Meh…

No one understood my struggles, so it was really hard to talk to anyone about them. Kids at school always turned up their noses at foul scents, and I knew it was me. I never raised my arms, even though I knew you could already see the sweat stains that were developing on my already wet shirt.

Name a deodorant!… I've tried it, both men and women brands. Potato peels under the arm, done! Lime under my arm… that too! Baking soda…washing my shirt every day! The tissue under the arm, a towel under the arm, pads under the arm, two shirts, three shirts, four shirts, I think you get the picture. So, I settled with wearing dark sweaters regardless of the weather.

My shoes never really lasted because my feet kept growing. I had already passed my mother's shoe size! Whew, it was real.

I was always teased about how big my feet were for a little girl. I was accustomed to just laughing it off, but secretly I wished it would just stop.

I wore shoes that always looked huge because of the struggle to find nice shoes in my size. I resorted to squeezing my giant feet into little shoes, I was in so much pain, but I found a temporary fix.

It felt like I was in a warzone, battling with many different opponents. At the age of seven, I remember watching my mom look at herself in the mirror, braids tied up, perfect skin as she prepared for bed. She examined her face, and I began to mimic her.

I vividly remember using my mom's blue soap by accident. The soap was the same color as mine, and I got complimented on the "clearing of my skin." Jokingly her friend that complimented me asked if I was using my mom's stuff. Silly me ran to grab the soap and said, "no, I use this soap!" They all laughed as they explained to me that it was my mom's toning soap.

I didn't know how to process that experience because I still didn't fully understand the toning process. After that day, I started toning my skin, seeing if it would make me prettier, get rid of the hideous ring around my lips, and clear the marks I had from acne. As a little girl, I wanted to hear that I was beautiful. I wish I could tell you that I grew out of it, but I didn't. I started looking for affirmation and acceptance in all of the wrong places.

My perception of who I was and what I thought of myself started to take shape during those years. My family reinforced my insecurities; they always said things like I wasn't shaped like my mom or didn't look like my friends. This all contributed to the idea of me not being enough. Those were the seeds that were planted, and that very seed grew with age. Each time I was told about my big feet, skin, and physique, the seed of insecurity continued to grow. What's crazy is, I didn't even realize what was happening. I laughed it off when I was made fun of because, as a child, it wasn't a big deal. It was all fun and games. It was a joke; my family and "friends" weren't trying to intentionally hurt me. It was a fact - they were making an observation, right?

WRONG!

Break Free Key – *Stop making excuses for those that hurt you (although it may not be intentional or can be characterized as innocent). Prioritize how it made you feel over what their intentions were to avoid caging scenarios.*

As unfortunate as it was, they were laughing at God's creation. They were laughing at His image and likeness according to Genesis 1:27, but I wasn't aware of it at the time. There was no framework or foundation that I could ground myself in; all I had were my negative thoughts and everyone's opinions. I knew as much as I was exposed to, and I was exposed to everything that was wrong with me.

"What do you know about yourself?"

"Where does it stem from?"

Ask yourself these questions, really think and reflect on how you view yourself?

As I got older, "girl talk" dissipated; the girls were still "the girls," but everyone seemed to be traveling down different paths.

I was a teenager in high school with a hell of a lot going on.

My feet stopped growing at size ten, thank God! I still sucked my bottom lip, and the ring around my lip was even darker than before. My boobs surely grew, but I still had my plywood figure. I still perspired, and my peers were sure to alert me and everyone else around me. They made songs and poems about my appearance, and of course, you know they gathered together in their cliques and mocked me. I had a crush or two that wouldn't give me the time of day. I mean, who was I kidding! I didn't look like any of my other friends, but a girl sure could dream right?

My hair was all over the place in high school. I was on a quest to fit in, so I started using products just because. I started coloring, flat ironing, burning and doing all kinds of things that led to my hair eventually just dropping all off. I said to everyone that I had just gotten a trim - that was my story, and I was sticking to it.

The things we do...right? Ugh!

There was something different about me in my senior year of high school. I decided to grow my hair naturally with no chemicals. It seemed to be going fine until it came down to graduation. As everyone started to prepare for their photos, the majority of my classmates talked about getting their hair wrapped or pressed.

Of course, I went into an instant panic because I just recently attended a baby dedication, and my hair was a TOTAL MESS! Yo, I looked cray-cray. (that's crazy if you weren't sure what cray meant) I knew I didn't want my photos to look like those photos from the baby dedication. After all, I was graduating, so this was huge. I decided that I would get a wrap since all of the other girls were doing it, but I would get it weaved in so it would be nicer and fuller since my hair was recovering from all of the damage prior. The only thing was I didn't own weave, but my mom did; I begged her over the next few days to use her Beautyrama extensions. This was her "good hair" at the time. She initially refused; however, time was winding down, and she finally said yes!

Funny enough, after all of that, I hated it when it was done. I had never gotten my hair wrapped or weaved in before; the way it looked on me didn't look like how I imagined it would or how it looked on other girls. What else could I have done? I had no idea what I would do with my hair, so I was stuck with it. And just like that my moment was ruined.

I got to school and was asked by the headmistress to make some adjustments, or I wouldn't be allowed to take my photos due to a strip of brown in my hair as a highlight - I guess she wasn't feeling it. A friend of mine had to pull the track out and tried to make me look slightly decent by giving me a press. However, the hair that I had borrowed from my mom was weighed down with products that she used previously.

Of course, I didn't know or think to wash it or even ask if she did.

What did I know?

I wanted to cry; all of this happened literally before I took my photos. It was a hot mess; I was a hot mess, and that experience showed in my esteem and on the photos. Once I got the photos, I hid them because I hated them. I made up some stories about what happened to them when my family asked.

Given the circumstances when graduation rolled around, I was back at square one with no idea of what to do because weave was not an option this time, and my natural hair wasn't cutting it. I ran around my neighborhood looking for a relaxer which seemed like the logical and realistic thing to do. This was my big day, and I just wanted to feel and look special. I got my hair relaxed and curled, which didn't turn out the way I had hoped (in comparison to what I'd seen on others), but it wasn't as bad as the other two occasions; so, I was okay. I felt pretty, and that was what mattered to me most.

When I think about it, it amazes me how a person's countenance changes depending upon how they feel. I didn't just graduate that day; something changed for me. And it all started with the way I felt. I didn't realize this then. It all came down to my foundation and the way I was trained. Like a sponge, I soaked up everything around me. What are you soaking up that has contributed to the way you see yourself or feel about yourself? It's not your fault, just like it wasn't mine - our sense of self is shaped during our childhood. Children tend to pick up ideals that they observe from their parents, neighbors, or even from television.

We must have the right foundation. Your foundation should be of love, light, and most importantly, it needs to be strong enough to withstand the elements of life because challenges and tests will come. Although I am writing this book years later, I still experience moments that I did during my childhood, but my foundation is different. I can now put my confidence in the fact that I am beautifully and wonderfully made. I'm not what people think of me; I am who God created me to be. As we continue this uncaging journey, I hope you are prepared to put in the work that is required to experience your release.

Put your money where your mouth is and
repeat after me!

I am

amazingly,

beautifully,

fearfully,

and

wonderfully

made.

THE ESCAPE

I thought that after high school, everything would fall into place or make sense. Soon I realized that this wasn't the case. I still struggled with my body: what it was doing and not doing. It felt like it was just acting out, only if it could get a grip.

I didn't pay much attention to people's comments and opinions of me; I was living life on my terms. I kept it moving. I wanted to get a tattoo or piercing as a birthday gift and a treat to myself since I secured my first job and had been working for a year. Although I was working, I was still required to give my entire paycheck to my stepdad, and I couldn't tell you what was done with the money. As a young lady, I was excited to get a job that would assist me in taking care of myself. I wanted to go for lunch with friends, get my hair and possibly my nails done, a cute outfit or two, or at least purchase my own feminine products, but I was robbed of that right.

I was turning eighteen, and out of respect, I told my parents of my decision to get either a navel piercing or a tattoo. My argument was that if I got a navel piercing, I would be able to take it out, whereas a tattoo would be there forever. I wanted to do this for myself and when I asked my parents the answer was "no." As a young adult, I felt like getting a tattoo or piercing was not that bad, nor as deep as they were making it seem. I still got it without them knowing, and let's just say it didn't go so well.

I found myself being asked to take out the ring that I wanted so badly. After a little white lie about the ring not being able to come out, I was told to get the plyers from the shed. I remember strolling straight past the shed and power walking to my best friend's house with just the clothing on my back - I don't even think I had on a bra. Traumatized, I knew my best friend would be the first place they'd look for me, and I was not in the mood to be found.

That night I stayed at my aunt's house; she was out of town having a baby, and had given me the keys earlier that month to keep an eye on the place while she was away. So, I thought it would be the perfect place to lay low until I figured out what I would do next. I was mortified at the thought of going back home; as the evening wore on, I heard a car pull up into my aunt's yard. I looked through the window only to see my mom and stepdad opening the car door, and the moment they stepped out of their vehicle, there was an instant power outage. Not just at my aunt's house but throughout the entire neighborhood.

They walked around the house to the back door, trying to get into the house. I tip-toed and stepped into the bathroom tub, being as quiet as possible. I heard them say, "looks like no one is home," and they walked back to their car. I saw the car lights flick on, and they drove off. Seconds after, the electricity came back on. At that moment, I took that incident as confirmation that I was doing the right thing.

Leaving home was the first radical yet self-fulfilling decision I've ever made in my entire life. It was the decision of doing something for myself for once. It was so much more than me just leaving home, but it was me breaking out and finally being free from the ideals and scripts that didn't help me be the young woman I felt I had to explore. Although I wasn't her exactly when I left, I had the freedom and ability to discover who I was and who I could be. At my aunt's house, I did all of the things I felt I should have already experienced as a young adult and even further a young woman. I was behind, and I had all intentions of catching up on all that I had missed out on.

I went to a party for the first time aside from my high school graduation party, which was technically my first party where I had to leave at 9 pm (the party was just getting started when I left). I stayed out with my friends for the first time, wore makeup for the first time, wore heels for the first time and bought an entirely new outfit for the first time. I was finally exploring what I liked and disliked, who I wanted to be, what I wanted to wear and how I wanted to feel.

I was finally able to express myself freely.

I wholeheartedly believe that I should have been able to experience all of these things, especially since I wasn't the type of girl that gave her parents trouble. I was focused, graduated top five in high school, but even after graduating, I still didn't have the freedom I desired.

Break Free Key – *Evaluate what is holding you back from exploring you and why it's holding you back for you to step into the queen you are meant to be.*

The truth is nothing is ever really what it seems. I was a girl in the body of an adult trying to figure out how to be myself. After high school, I was seen as always put together and well-shaped but was still empty, still lost, and still trying to put the pieces of me together. I even had a boyfriend who would always tell me how good-looking I was and affirmed me, but there was still this barrier that no one seemed to breakthrough.

To understand the transition and the journey to my uncaging and, in turn, start your own uncaging, I have to tell you that the only way I saw and started to experience a breakthrough was when I made a drastic move. At that moment, I developed a new way of thinking and being... heck; a whole new way of doing. I took the leap of faith and made a step toward what I wanted, not knowing what would come out of it, which was extremely scary, but what was scarier was being caught in the cycle of never enough. It was not my style, and predictability didn't exactly look good on me. There's just something about the unknown that can be so freeing and liberating. Having tasted freedom created a lane for me to shift my thoughts and actions. I no longer wanted to be that little girl that surrounded herself with the bars, namely by what people said about me and what I internalized with each word and feeling associated with all that was said.

Sticks and bones may break my bones, but your words were the bars that surrounded me.

What is surrounding you? Because something is, I know that because I didn't realize how bad it was for me until it got bad.

It's interesting that even though the bars surrounded me, I stuck them into the ground and made sure that they were secured. I secured these bars by agreeing with the words that came out of the mouth of those that said I wasn't enough or I couldn't. There were instances when I would sometimes beat them to it and say it about myself before they did since it was coming anyway. Am I the only one that does that?

Have you ever done that? With every move, are you confronted by a bar that either you or someone has placed before you?

In order for us to walk into the fullness of who we are, we sometimes have to be ready to make the hard decisions.

It's never easy. That's why it's a hard decision, but know that you'll thank yourself for it once you get through the rough patch - it's smooth sailing moving forward. Hard decisions get easier when you prioritize yourself, your growth, and your happiness.

Are you ready to move if you have to? Can you get rid of the toxic people in your life that aren't adding value to you? Get rid of the old habits, environments, and any baggage that may be holding you back from yourself. I know what you're thinking, "what does it matter?"

The old and new cannot cohabit! Why? Well, I'm glad you asked. Do you mix your dirty laundry with your clean laundry? No! What will happen is that the dirt and odor from the dirty laundry take over the clean ones and become dirty! Therefore, if anyone is in Christ, he is a new creation; old things have passed away; behold, all things have become new. 2 Corinthians 5:17 NKJV

The same applies here when you're trying to hold onto the old parts of your life that are now dirty because you've worn them; they've been exposed to the elements, and they can't cohabit with your newness.

This is when we have to separate ourselves just like we separate our laundry. Sometimes it just requires us to give ourselves a good washing, and in some instances, we have to get rid of the pieces that we've outgrown. It's normal to do away with the old, to make space for the new. We must apply this concept not just with our clothes but with our lives too! Besides, why would you want to hold on to the old when the new is bigger and better? The significance of my shift was that I was walking away from the old and walking into my new. That was my big move, my hard decision, the shift I needed. No longer comfortable with being fed what I should feel or what I should be doing through the bars cemented by everyone else.

What do you need to walk away from?

Are you allowing your old to stink up your new?

Like me, you may not be aware of the cycles you're in because you are so accustomed to that environment. Darling, you need to break free and get out! I didn't recognize the stench because I'd been sitting in it for so long, I got accustomed to the scent. I had to make a conscious decision to walk away from the environment that was negatively impacting me to realize that I had gotten used to the smell of it. So, here's to being aware of the smell of life, separating the clean from the dirty, and occasionally doing away with what doesn't fit.

Put your money where your mouth is and repeat after me!

I make room

for the

new things

in my life

which are

always

bigger &

better.

SEEKING TRUTH

The process of allowing yourself to be shaped while embracing the good, bad and ugly is quite interesting. As I started to navigate through this process, I started to ask myself some important questions. I was on a quest to find out who I was, what I wanted, and who I ultimately wanted to become.

God has a strategic way of turning our lives around and working things out for our good. I once believed that I was a deeply flawed individual and that God used the very things that I despised - to catapult me into purpose.

It all started with my cousin practically begging me to attend a meeting with her. I stopped by her home to say hi, and I didn't have any plans, so I agreed. We went to Forest Heights Academy in a classroom to the left. I'm racking my brain right now as I'm writing, trying to remember whether my cousin had mentioned what the meeting was about. Nonetheless, I do remember walking into the classroom and sitting down and looking around. I whispered under my breath, "Oh, modeling, she wants to be a model. Cool!"

That day I wore a brown t-back tank top, jeans, and brown boots. The instructors looked at me and asked if I would be interested in giving them a hand since I was just sitting and watching. The instructor changed the music and motioned to me to join the young ladies who were walking in pairs.

As I looked hesitantly, I noticed there was a missing person and that my cousin was walking by herself. So, I decided to help and just walked! I wasn't as prepared as the other girls, including my cousin, who definitely looked the part. But I was just doing it for fun. I walked back and forth in the classroom until my feet were sore from being on my tippy toes. I didn't have on heels to walk in, and even though I was just helping, I was still required to walk like a model.

At the end of the meeting, the instructor and my cousin surrounded me in their successful attempt to have me join the Miss Abaco Pageant. I remember agreeing after my cousin indicated that having a familiar face there would help. "We can do it together," she noted.

BOOM... and just like that, I was in my first pageant; there you have it, folks. I was completely bamboozled.

I had no idea what entering a pageant would mean for me. But I knew that it involved a transformation based on Miss Congeniality - a transformation that involved money, money that I didn't have at the time. Remember, I just left home and was on my own. I had just started a new job and was living in my aunt's living room. Money was TIGHT!

I had no coach, no training, I was in over my head, but I showed up anyway. I mean, I didn't have an excuse as to why I couldn't. My aunt literally lived less than five minutes away from where rehearsals were taking place.

I was the first at rehearsals, and I vividly remember sitting there talking myself out of me being there. I didn't see what my nineteen-year-old self had to offer. I had nothing to show for my nineteen years of being on this earth, and I thought it was pointless. I did graduate from high school, found a job, and didn't get pregnant, although persons in my community thought that I would have. Well, ha-ha, in your face!

I was surrounded by other beautiful women who boasted about their modeling experiences, the contests they've won, and I honestly became intimidated.

I compared myself to the others because I've never participated in fashion shows or contests. I wasn't experienced and I had no exposure, which caused me to doubt my ability to compete. I felt small, and I already questioned why I was even there to begin with - they had enough girls. I wish I could say it got better, but it didn't.

Break Free Key – *What you nurture is what will continue to grow. Which thoughts are you feeding? It's easy to think of all of the reasons why you can't do something or why you aren't good enough. Those thoughts only flood our minds when we are comparing ourselves to others. We start to compare our worth, abilities, and accomplishments; remember that we all have a special race to run that requires something different from each of us. So, nurture what you have and forget what you don't. If you don't have it, you don't need it. You have exactly what you need for the season you're in; you just need to make it work for you.*

My pageantry experience intensified. We had our official photoshoot literally after our unveiling: it was the public event that showcased the contestants competing officially. I felt the pressure, and at that very moment, I felt ugly and insecure. The voice of my director didn't make me feel any better. It was obvious that I didn't appear on camera the way the other girls did. I didn't get the "yes, beautiful, amazing, good, like the others.

My perception changed that night. The fire ignited in me and I decided not to accept the feeling of not being enough. I came up with a strategy to show everyone that I could be successful at pageantry, and our first official appearance would be the place to do that. We arrived at the annual Christmas bazaar held in Marsh Harbour every year. I soon realized that the island was not knowledgeable of how a full-blown pageant was supposed to run. The reigning queen had been appointed the year before, and the organization was just getting its bearings. I quickly noticed the fan-favorite; however, I tried not to pay that much attention to it because this was my time to shine. We all stood on stage with all eyes on us, and one at a time, we said our name, age, and gem (the theme of the pageant was island gem, and we represented various gems).

As each girl went up and completed their introduction, I studied them and began to break down as I compared myself to each girl that went before me and the crowd's response. As soon it was my turn, I said, "Nyisha Tilus, nineteen, diamond," and instead of resounding applause like the others, I literally could hear a handful of claps. I fell back into the line and wanted the stage to open up and swallow me. We exited the stage, and the crowd cheered and called the names of contestants they came to support.

I looked in the crowd, and there was not one family member there to support me or cheer me on. Mentally, I checked out and was ready to go home. The only thing hindering me was the fact that I was hiking a ride. I continued to compare myself to the other delegates, and mesyé (the head director) didn't help with his criticism about my speech, tone, and at that point, I didn't care to open my mouth again. It wasn't about how I looked this time, but I was being made fun of because of the way I sounded naturally.

As much as I wanted to and tried, I couldn't escape speaking; it was a part of the job. What I didn't get was how it made me feel. It felt like I was putting up more bars. It didn't get better, and I questioned my space in the pageant. There was another public appearance happening, and I dreaded going. We were required to make another introduction to the public and complete a pitch challenge selling a piece of jewelry from the jewelry store where the event was taking place... double whammy, sheesh!

The thought of the challenge was horrifying. I thought to myself, "if I couldn't introduce myself, how could I sell a product?" We were given time to work on our pitch, and of course, I had nothing aside from my name and the name of the product. I drew a total blank, I walked around the store looking for inspiration, and each aisle I turned through was a contestant writing and me just standing there like, "why am I not writing?" Time was up, and we each had to pitch to the store owners, customers, and the media. One by one, the girls went up and sold the product, and I faded. It was my turn, and one thing led to another, and the next thing I knew, I choked.

I heard a few people say, "keep going." There were faint claps for encouragement, but it was time to get away from the spotlight. I ended by saying some fluff and ran off the stage.

I didn't win the challenge, and I left that event feeling defeated. I truly did not care to be bothered anymore. I thought to myself, "I'm not cut out for this." Some people made me question whether or not I wanted to participate in the pageant, but I was too far into it to turn back now. The feelings and turmoil I went through were very real; I still remember it even to this day. We were asked to speak again, but this time on our platform at rehearsal. I needed to determine which cause I would go with since there were four areas that I was passionate about. Deciding which one was going to be my platform was difficult. The platform options were Disabled Individuals, Cancer, Self-esteem Development, and Domestic Violence.

All four of these areas were very dear and near to my heart. One of my four brothers was diagnosed with downs-syndrome. He had been back and forth to hospitals for seven years of his life.

I understood what depression looked and felt like. I know how it feels to doubt myself and believe that no one loves me. I know how it feels to be in a dysfunctional and abusive home. I know how it felt to be overwhelmed with so many emotions after finding out my mother was struck with cancer. I felt the weight of each of those causes on my shoulders; they all weighed on me like never before.

I called my mom to get her perspective; we hadn't spoken for months (since I left home) up until I found out she had cancer. Let me just say here it's far more complicated, but I wanted to be there for her after I found out about her illness, so I made it a point to reconcile, patch things up, and include her in this journey with me to have her think about anything other than her illness. I called her, and I instantly discern the uncertainty and hesitation in her voice.

I immediately knew she probably had one of those days... that's what I use to call it when I was little. The call from my mom made my mind up for me; my platform was going to be domestic violence awareness. My mother wouldn't stand up for herself, but that didn't mean that I couldn't stand up for her. At that moment, it became personal, both the platform and the pageant. By promoting domestic violence as my platform, I became the voice of my mom, and I needed to talk; I wanted to talk. It became so much bigger than me. When I told my mom what I was going to do on that same call, she said, "Thank you!"

I felt a tremendous sense of content. We hung up, and I was on fire. It became my determination to do this for her, if for no one else. I was ready to do whatever I had to help people like her that were going through domestic violence, thinking they were all alone. My experience in the pageant instantly shifted; it didn't matter anymore whether I was made fun of or whether someone thought I shouldn't be there.

As the competition went on, I remember feeling hurt and devasted when my mom never showed up to any of my events. I wanted my mom to be there. I wanted to be able to reach out to her. She never showed up because she was worried about what her then husband would think and how he would react. This made me feel like she was choosing him over me...again. Rehashing all of these feelings was not easy, but I was determined that I would not quit my quest. I wanted to, but I had to finish.

I began to think about the things I had gone through as a little girl, watching my mom, brothers, and even myself being abused physically, mentally, and emotionally. I wanted my voice to be heard now more than ever, and I did not care who heard it as long as the ones that needed to did. I didn't care what my stepdad thought, what he'd do to me, or whether anyone would make fun of the way I spoke. I'd just keep talking because I realized it's the silence that restrains us. Speak up for yourself; when you stay silent and keep everything inside, those emotions begin to fester. You become angry, aggressive, and you project those feelings onto other people. For the first time in my life, I was doing what I thought I was meant to do when I shared my story to inspire and encourage others. The competition is coming down to the final hours, and we start to prepare. All of the contestants are at the salon getting pre-curled, a few of the girls and I make a stop to a party with curlers in our hair and then head home to rest up for the big day less than twenty hours away.

Four hours into I guess what could be called my beauty rest, I get a call. I'm not sure if I want to relive that experience in its entirety, but a dear friend who the girls and I had just seen at the party had just been in an accident, and one of the contestants who I was close with was on her way to pick me up to see if he was okay. We get to the hospital to hear screaming, and at that moment, we looked at each other and knew. He was gone. It was a long night. We stayed there for a bit to give support where we could have; our community was extremely tight-knit - everyone knew everyone, not to mention the young man that passed away was a true community angel, so we all felt this blow to the gut.

I got home and couldn't sleep. I pinched myself, hoping it was a dream. But it wasn't. In less than four hours, I needed to be up and back to the salon to finish prep for the pageant that was in the next eight hours. We go there to find that it was at the wall of that same salon our dear friend had crashed. We stood waiting for the owners to open up and could see his blood just there. I couldn't stop crying; I closed my eyes, hoping it would all go away, it'll stop someway somehow. I hadn't felt this much pain since my uncle passed.

Everyone kept telling me, along with the other contestant with me, to stop crying. But they didn't understand, and even if we did for a second, tears would automatically start to flow down my face and then hers. I needed to stand on a stage and perform and do this thing that he had just wished us the best of luck on. I could barely keep my makeup on as the tears streamed down my face. I was trying my best to keep it together as volunteers tried to reassure me. The volunteers coached me on and reminded me that my dear friend would've wanted me to continue with the pageant. I couldn't believe he was gone. I was so out of it that during the opening number, the contestant next to me told me to go, and I walked off the stage before it was even finished.

I remember wearing this white gown and feeling this sense of heaviness even though the fabric was literally as light as can be with a cut out on the right side that added to a sense of airiness.

At the end of the night, I had made it to the top five. As much as I wanted to go beyond that point, I wasn't giving it my all; I was just going through the motions. It didn't change the heaviness I felt that night. I was upset that I didn't do as well as I would have liked, upset in the sense that I thought I let him down.

I'm sure that was a whole lot to take in because it was a whole lot to write. So, I got you.

But there is one important message I want you to get from my overall Miss Abaco experience in the three situations I've shared with you.

Firstly, when you start to compare yourself, you lose yourself and sight of the purpose you're being directed to. Even when you're doing your thing, anything is bound to happen. The path to success isn't a straight line. There are bumps in the road, signs that can send you in the wrong direction depending on how you read them, and accidents that can take you completely off course. It's all a part of life and the journey. I was lost, found, then completely thrown off, stretched, and then some.

The experiences of life won't all be positive ones, and that's okay. They won't all feel good, and that's okay. In some cases, you may not want to do them, and that's just fine because they're all a part of your story. There are many pieces to the puzzle: the good, bad, and ugly pieces that you've tried to fit into other parts where it doesn't belong. Here's the kicker though, once you complete a puzzle, you look at it and then show off what you did. The fact that you completed that puzzle inspires others to try the puzzle out too. Your story, your puzzle, is not your own! It's your experience, and you do put the pieces together, yes, but it's really for the person you need to show it off to so that they can put their puzzle together too.

You need to put the puzzle of your life together so that you can encourage the persons you're called to show it to. That's why you can't get caught up in comparing yourself to another piece that fits perfectly somewhere else. They were uniquely designed for that space just like you are uniquely designed for a space. Yes, you tried a few spaces prior that may have caused some damage because it looked like it was the right fit and ended up being all wrong. I know it hurts, but I need you to acknowledge that pain and that area of opportunity. For me, my area of opportunity was speaking. However, when I let go of the expectations of others and even the limitations I placed on myself, I found my voice when the enemy was trying to shut me up. You have to be on your game! You're in a cage because you've allowed someone to place you in a cage and lock the gate. But one thing remains, the only way you're going to get out is if you make up in your mind that YOU ARE GOING TO GET OUT!

Break Free Key - *Ensure that the puzzle of your life is waterproof. Let the words just roll right off. Don't let it sink through and leave watermarks, stains, and damage you. The ball is in your court just like it's always been in mine. You have to make the decision; you have the final say. Even God doesn't tell you what to do. He gives you your options and free will and says decide...death or life. So, choose wisely. Choose what you accept, choose the life you want, choose how you want to feel, choose yourself every time.*

Put your money where your mouth is and
repeat after me!

I decide

what

I want

for me

and my

life.

AWAKENED TRUTH

Appreciating what is because of what was is an interesting occurrence. I've found that this only happens when you spend time with yourself, and most importantly, you spend time with God; this process requires you to be open.

It's an awkward series of events, but it's vital when it comes to gaining perspective. You know what I mean, we do it all the time when we compare the current partner in our lives to the ones prior and literally laugh and wonder... "what was I thinking?" That kind of awkwardness gives you a sense of increased awareness of where you are because of where you've been. And there I was in this self-conscious stage, yet growing as I reflected.

I had to consider whether I wanted to view life through the lens of half full or half empty and be honest with myself about where I was.

I knew that I was a full kind of girl, always optimistic, but conversely, the point is to always look at the context.

In some instances, that can be found in what is going on presently, while in other instances, it can be found in what has already occurred; either way, you gain the right amount of insight and sense of direction for what's next. There was so much that I still needed to work through after my first pageant. Acknowledging what I needed to, accepting what I had to, and doing away with all of the rest that wasn't serving any purpose.

I passed through a series of thoughts, emotions, and actions that weren't all that pleasant but necessary. I recognized the feeling of sadness from not doing as well as I would've liked in the pageant.

I accepted the reality that my last name came with disapproval, so the negativity I received because of it wasn't personal. Therefore, I did away with it and went on with my life.

A life where "nothing was the same" in the words of Sir Drake.

After the pageant, I lost my job due to my unexpected unavailability for work. I had no idea pageantry could be so demanding. But the icing on the cake for my boss was when I couldn't get on a flight back home for my shift after a weekend trip, a trip that was needed in more ways than one; it took a load off after attending my dear friend's funeral and competing in a pageant.

I had a lot going on (and needed to get away for a bit). Still, my boss had a business to run, so I completely understood what was happening and why. Even when he didn't have to, he compensated me for my time there, which wasn't that long... BEST BOSS EVER!

A few weeks later, I was homeless; my aunt and I weren't seeing eye to eye on quite a bit, so that environment was a no-no for me. I left and asked a family friend if I was able to crash at her place until I got a job, and she agreed. I did get a job...thank God, however, that family friend ended up asking me to leave like a month in because she thought I was a bad influence on her daughter.

(Sips tea...it wasn't me)

So, there I was, homeless again. I didn't want to move back in with my grandmother because I felt I had outgrown the community where she lived, where I once lived too. I needed to continue to move forward and not back. It had nothing to do with forgetting where I came from but more to do with not running back to comfort when things got tough. I was determined to stay the course regardless of how difficult it was. Moving back with my aunt was a definite no, and moving back with my mom and stepdad was a HELL TO THE NO!

I could feel the tears run down my face as I sat in my work staff meeting thinking, "where the hell am I going to go?" as I read the text message sent to me by that family friend about having to leave, my supervisor looked at me and motions for me to meet her outside; I explained what was happening and one thing led to another which resulted in me now crashing at her boss' place who just so happened to be the aunt of the guy that I was seeing at the time.

Since both her kids were off to college, she had two spare rooms. I moved in that evening, and literally a week or two into it, I had to leave because she was at that Stella getting her groove back phase in her life. It was awkward walking into the place right in the middle of her having a date or trying to get to know someone.

I love her for trying though; she was definitely a sweetheart.

Luckily, we had discussed a prior plan, and I ended up moving into my very first apartment all by myself...above my church. Things were finally looking up; I saw and felt the shift. My best friend from Nassau moved in with me, so I had company. I ended up getting a call from my old boss (the job from the pageant) who was hiring and thought since I already knew the organization and he could trust me, that he would just hire me...again. There I was, working two jobs, had my own apartment, and was in the process of getting a car.

I turned into Stella and started getting my groove back, a groove that I didn't even realize I had. It took me a while to figure it out, to understand that I wasn't the average Jane...I wasn't your average chick, even though I believed I was for a long time.

I put the pieces of myself together, and for the first time, I had the pieces in the right places.

After being traumatized, experiencing hurt, and doing some hurting myself, I started dancing to the beat of my own drum, and I LIKED IT!

Just when things started looking up, my boss decided to shut down his company. I wasn't too happy about it obviously, but he needed to do what he needed to.

Before closing officially, I applied for college, which was a big deal. A few months prior, I told my best friend college was for the birds, and there I was running around trying to get references and my paperwork together. My other job was experiencing a slow season. I found myself having to move again, and I found another apartment. This one was more modern and spacious, and it was all mine! The tectonic plates of my life were finally coming together, it wasn't easy, but it was necessary. Some shaking did occur, but the shock and alignment that was taking place were what my mind, body, and soul needed.

Break Free Key – *It may not go the way you expect it to go, but know that it is going exactly how it is supposed to go. Trust the process, trust the lessons life has taught you; all of them will help with the obstacles life decides to place in your way. You've been prepared to take them on.*

All of this chaos led me to a whole other island of The Bahamas, Nassau.

Crazy right!?

Another big move.

It was like I was moving to the big apple of The Bahamas to pursue my degree, the first degree in my family. This was a big deal for me, but it wasn't all roses in the garden, though. I didn't leave home in the best of terms, and now more than ever, I needed a change in scenery. I needed to be exposed to more and broaden my horizons. And this was my chance to see what was out there.

Pageants were nowhere on my radar, nowhere in my vocabulary, until one day at school, one of my professors asked me, "why don't you do Miss Bahamas?" My response was instantly, "Well, I did Miss Abaco," I guess at that time to indicate I had done one pageant, so I did them all.

HA!

Boy, was I wrong.

After that day, I started seeing pageants everywhere. They were on my social media; they were in the newspaper, I mean everywhere. One day my best friend's aunt and I started talking about the beauty industry; she was a model, and I didn't consider myself one because I didn't think I was what they wanted. We sat and discussed wanting to change the beauty industry, changing and shaping the idea of beauty and the fact that there is no one standard of beauty. We created this pact to do a pageant together in 2015. At this time, I had just lost my job again, but this time in Nassau, and was trying to find my way. So, there it was again me and the thought of pageantry.

I eventually found a job shortly after our pact and became close with one of my co-workers who wanted to be a model, and I wanted to continue with pageantry; in our minds, it worked! I purchased a camera and took photos of her to help build up her modeling portfolio, and she assisted me with my pageantry endeavors. I started exercising to prepare my body and build up endurance. I gained about 30+ pounds, and I was determined to drop the weight.

There were tons of things going on in the background, I finally purchased my own car, my best friend moved to Abaco and was in the process of moving to Cuba for school, and I was now transitioning from living with my best friend's mom to the place I was originally supposed to live at when I moved to Nassau. It just so happens that it would be with the mom of my existing boyfriend. She and I developed a relationship before her son and I started dating. Our relationship grew into something really beautiful, to the point where everyone thinks that she's my biological mom. During the early morning hours one day, she walked into my room and woke me up. She said the Lord told her to wake me up, and that we needed to start exercising to prepare for my pageant.

LIKE WOAHH!!

I had never told her about doing another pageant or that I was even interested in pageantry, for that matter. I sat up flabbergasted, I had no words, and I did just as she said. We began exercising, and I went to the gym with a crown in mind.

Some months later, we weren't as consistent as we were in the initial stages. I started to get a tad bit unfocused and demotivated. I picked up a black and white notebook titled "The Journey." In it, I wrote all of my thoughts, ideas, goals, and plans; as I went through the book, I realized that I was basically out of pages and literally tossed the book to the side on the top of some laundry. Later that day, I went to a mid-day service at Global Harvest. There was a guest speaker this particular Wednesday. I will never forget this day; the guest speaker imparted the message and went into prophecy. He looked at me and said, "that book that you looked at & tossed to the side, God says everything in that book will come to pass this year."

My mind was blown! No one knew about my book, definitely not this guy, and he was spot on. I sat down in my seat, and he walked over to me and said, "you should probably rest your feet and ankles for now because you'll be doing a lot of walking in heels." I immediately thought about the journey to the crown, and a light switch turned on. After that word, I made arrangements to get back in the gym and created a regimen.

Some weeks later, I saw an advertisement for Miss University of The Bahamas. No, it wasn't Miss Bahamas, but it was the perfect training ground for Miss Bahamas. Your thoughts and perceptions truly do shape your journey. I could have very well disregarded all that I had been through and say, why would I want to go through this again. I could have told the preacher guy, that sounds nice, but it didn't happen when I thought it would; so, I don't want it anymore. It's so important to move with context because the context will allow you to stay the course.

The context will have you reminding yourself of the goal even when it doesn't look like it's possible. It will remind you of the promise made to you. As well as hold you accountable for what it is you said you wanted to do and be.

What do you need to remind yourself of?

Pour back into yourself even when you start to feel down, you're running on empty, and it's time to fill up and get up and keep moving.

It's not easy; it comes with some uncomfortable feelings. I know; remember what I did after going through the journey book?

I tossed it because I started to feel inadequate, I started to feel like I was useless, I started to feel like I wasn't able to accomplish the goals I had set out for myself; however, in the same instance of feeling that way, I went where I could be reminded again.

I went to the place where I knew I could re-up. The place where I needed to be reminded of not just what I thought about myself but what God said and His thoughts of me. The truest and purest form of me.

As a follower of Christ, I believed that when I went through the book, my subconscious and my spirit knew that I was running on empty and needed to be filled; my spirit which knew and remembered the promise but needed to get the rest of me to the place where I wasn't caught up on my flesh, the surface and what was going on around me naturally. My spirit knew I had written it all down and made it plain. In an attempt to remind me (mind, body, and spirit), my spirit believed but my mind and body didn't, so I tossed the book. My mind and body were focused on what I was seeing and feeling presently, whereas my spirit focused on what I was going to be despite that. So, my spirit led me to the place where my flesh wouldn't be able to flourish. It had to come to the subjection of the spirit, where I can be reminded that it wasn't by my might but God's.

Where is that place for you? We all have that place, whether we're aware of it or not. I know for me that place in the PRESENCE OF THE ALMIGHTY GOD.

After all, the bible says that it's not by might or power but by the spirit. Zechariah 4:6

What do you have to put under subjection? What thoughts? Feelings? Spirits?

Find a place or person to help you and remind you of the mission, the promise and the goal. We aren't meant to do life alone, and it's when I started including others in my journey and it changed for me. Sometimes you'll need help getting out of the cage.

Put your money where your mouth is and
repeat after me!

I will

not only

look around

but also

look above

to be filled.

TRAINING GRACE

On the 1st of February, the Miss University of the Bahamas pageant's announcement came out on social media. Having no idea where the opportunity would lead, all I knew was that it was my chance to get back into the saddle of pageantry. Win or lose, at the very least, I would have been a bit more prepared for Miss Bahamas. At that time, I had quite a few things going on in my life. I was in my senior year at University, I worked full-time, was trying to become a part of this particular thing, all while trying to have somewhat of social life.

In trying to map out how I would juggle these endeavors, I sought advice from key persons I thought would lead me to the path of success while on this journey; my mentor, advisor & professors so that the process would go smoothly as far as classes and assignments; some indicated that I was stretching myself too thin, but the decision would ultimately be mine to make.

While there was one more loose end that I needed to tie, I faced a wall when I was told flat out, "it's either this (thing) or that (the pageant). You can't do both."

At that moment, I immediately wanted this pageant even more; after all, no one tells me what I can't do!

It would have been a bit more palatable if they had suggested or presented their case as to why I shouldn't, but no one tells me what I can or can't do.

(It's my nobody puts baby in the corner vibe)

I decide that for myself.

I decided to go ahead and sign up for the pageant anyway! Competing nationally started to become something that I could see myself doing. I finally started to feel like I was worthy of a shot at the crown. Aside from that, I had just been told that everything in my "book" would come to pass. I felt like this was the perfect opportunity for me to prepare.

Additionally, the application fee was $75, which to me was unheard of, so I quickly filled my application out and paid the fee. By mistake or not, my spot was solidified.

Break Free Key - *Rather than second-guessing yourself and your decisions, learn to make the move and maneuver later. We can become so consumed by the implications of a decision that leads to talking ourselves out of it. Or we ask others for advice on a decision, and they talk us out of it. Whether we are the ones talking ourselves out of it or letting others do the talking, it's time to just do it, even if you're scared.*

Although my goal was to prepare for Miss Bahamas, I still would give Miss University of The Bahamas my everything. Most importantly I would be myself. I went through the training, and there were instances where I was afraid; I didn't feel as confident. The feelings from my last pageant started to resurface especially at our official photoshoot. Although it was a great day, during my actual photoshoot session, I got flustered. I wanted things to be different, but I thought about my shoot at my first pageant. I thought about things I heard people say about me, and I thought about how my photos in the past looked compared to others.

It all started to come back as I tried my best to shake it off and give it my all. Yet, I was having a hard time. My personality wasn't coming across in photos. My essence was getting lost in translation of who I was and what I was being asked to do.

The photographer said, "Well, that's not me, right!?

I think it's her; I think she's the problem!"

As I walked to the next session, videography, I was initially excited that a female was doing it. Naturally, I should have felt a bit more comfortable, but I wasn't.

It was the worst.

She asked me to be sexy, flirty, sassy, and I completely froze. All of the insecurities that I experienced when I was a little girl started to come back like a flood again. I didn't know how to be those things, and that was weird. It felt strange for me, but the other delegates that seemed to know exactly what it meant and what they were doing. I questioned whether or not I should be there but reminded myself of why I was there and the bigger goal. I was doing this for me, so it didn't matter what anyone else looked like, what type of dress they wore or hairstyle they had, or what specific compliments contestants received from the committee. I wasn't going down that road again. The process, although dreadful for me for personal reasons, wasn't all that bad. It was a bit easier with an organization that wasn't blatantly biased. They indicated when things didn't look right for all contestants. Now that, I can appreciate. They offered help, and the Lord knew I needed it. They ensured that the delegates were okay, which was exactly what I desired: a completely different experience. From that moment on, I knew that this pageant was going to be different.

I focused on what it was that I brought to the table and what it was that I would do once I got there. I worked on how I would present myself and ultimately how I would carry myself as the Queen I knew I was destined to be.

This became even more evident for me on the day of my unveiling. A day I will never forget, as I hastily strut through campus to make contestants call time after picking up my sister (cousin) and second mom to attend the event, I realized that my second mom wasn't next to me. I looked around for her and noticed that she was rushing, trying to catch up to my sister and me. As she walks up to me, she starts to explain that her scarf flew away and in trying to get it, a University employee felt the need to share with her a disagreement that just took place with other University employees over their discontent about students of Haitian descent participating in the pageant. She goes on to share that her colleagues thought that these students with these "funny last names" had no right to be in this pageant.

The holy indignation I felt right before walking into the holding room was unbelievable. I was one of those students, with the funny last names, I thought to myself, the nerve of these people.

What right did they have to tell me that I didn't belong? What right did they have to tell me that I could not compete or participate in a pageant at a University that I paid to attend like every other student there? That moment changed my life, I knew that I wasn't accepted because of my last name, but on the day of my unveiling, I vowed that I would show them that I was not going to change or water down who I was to be accepted by people that didn't want to accept me anyway. It was no longer about them or anyone else; it was about me, #ThatTilusGirl and the fact that I was worthy of my space and place. I was worthy and had every right to be where I wanted and to do what I wanted. With every training and rehearsal, I would give it 1000%. As we started to come down to competition time, I started to feel the pressure. I read what was being said on social media. I heard the little chitter-chatter here and there. Along with school and work, I started to feel and experience the weight of it all.

I felt overwhelmed. I remember sitting at a glass table and crying my eyes out because of the heaviness I experienced. I didn't know if I was able to carry it. I didn't know if I was doing the right thing because everything started to rush by. It felt like a mighty wind that I wasn't sure I could withstand.

I didn't want to quit, but I felt like I had to because of the external pressure I was experiencing in balancing all that was happening in my life at that time. As I sat at that glass table, I reflected on how much I wanted to be Miss Bahamas, and Miss University of The Bahamas wasn't that. So, it wouldn't have made a difference if I quit anyway, right? Crazy how our thoughts can spiral out of control sometimes. I immediately reminded myself of a promise I made to go after any and everything that I was fearful of. The mere fact that I started to experience fear meant that the enemy was trying to keep me away from whatever I was afraid of pursuing. Anytime I would start to experience fear or become fearful of a thing, I remembered that God didn't give me a spirit of fear! 2 Timothy 1:7, so if I was fearful of a thing, then it isn't God. So, I stayed in the pageant, dashed over to the venue for the top model competition that was happening less than 3 hours from my mid-pageant crisis. As much as I wanted clarity, I think I got my sign after I placed top three in the Top Model Competition, which was huge for me. So much so that I cried even more because I almost dropped out literally hours before. Had I not shown up, I would not have been there...I would not have placed...I would not have been in place for that thing with my name on it.

My mindset and attitude all changed. I was ready. I wasn't playing to play anymore; I was on a mission, which was the only thing on my mind.

The director of the organization posted a photo of the crown and sash in the contestants' WhatsApp group as I'm pulling out of the driveway to head to campus. I pulled back into the yard, ran into the house, and shouted, "Hey, look at my crown! It's here! It's here!"

Oh, how I admire that faith.

I think about the faith of David during this time when he fought against Goliath. He was ready to go, no questions, just stones.

Ready to go into battle with no question in his mind because he knew the promise; he knew who went before him. He was in place, ready to take on what God had for him. Imagine if David wasn't in position? I don't even want to think about it. There's something special about knowing you're right on time. Whether for an event, to pick up a package or for food.

I've always been a stickler for time, so go with me if you will, to the night that I almost missed my judges' interview because something I wasn't supposed to be doing anyway ate up my time. Before I go into what happened, let me say something, your time is priceless. You will never get it back. Once it's gone, it's gone! The next point I'll make is that if the enemy can't stop you, he will try to contain you. I was going full fledge with the pageant, so there was no stopping me. Hence, the enemy tried to contain and trap me in another way that would eventually almost cost me, and thank God it didn't.

I almost missed that interview which was 35% percent of our overall score.

Here I was, pulling up at the location for the interview, changing out of jeans and a t-shirt to my interview skirt set in a parking lot at almost 10 pm. It was too dark for me to put on makeup, and not to mention, I was extremely late. So much so I couldn't even chance squeezing in another minute to powder my face.

I looked up to see the director of the pageant looking out of the window; I automatically think he's looking for me. I rushed up the stairs holding back my tears. I got there, and I'm thankful that I asked for the last interview slot and how this could be a whole lot worse. I apologized for my tardiness and the director indicated that it was okay, and I went into the judges' room. I walk in to have a seat looking at 7 judges. I say my name, and they went right into their questions.

I shared my heart because that was all that I had. I didn't look the part at that moment. I wasn't feeling the part at that moment, but Miss University of The Bahamas wasn't just an outlet for me to prepare for Miss Bahamas anymore; it became something that I wanted. So, I shared what I wanted and hoped to do to build the University. I left my heart on that table and cried, but I kept going; I cried some more, but I kept going. I left that interview in more tears because I felt like I messed up.

> **Break Free Key** – *Don't focus on the past, acknowledge where you are presently, and adjust. When you take a wrong turn, you immediately gather yourself, figure out where you are and prepare to get back en route to your destination. Focus on what's to come. You can't change the past, but you can shape your future.*

We get to the final night, and I am ready; I'm ready for whatever is supposed to happen. I was calm, centered, and ready for whatever was to come and what came was the crown, sash, and the title of the first Miss University of The Bahamas 2017.

The little girl from a shantytown on an island, who hung with the boys and ran around barefooted, did that! My life has never been the same since that moment. All because I was in position, the University I attended wasn't my first choice; it was my last. What if I wasn't obedient to the advice to start at COB now UB? Who would be the first-ever Miss University of The Bahamas? What if I didn't start to prepare when Fany came into my room and said what she did about preparation? What if I wasn't in place, had I dropped out? There's always something good around the corner of obedience. Even when it doesn't look like it, we just need the faith to take the first step to uncover it. It won't be doing cartwheels and screaming, "look at me." Despite everything, "What is for you won't pass you if you're in place. STAY READY - then you won't have to get ready!

Put your money where your mouth is and
repeat after me!

I'm in

position

and

I'm prepared

for what

belongs to me.

TAILORED CROWN

Miss UB, that was me!

Ready to be the best ambassador that I knew I could be for my University. The most exciting opportunity I had as Miss University of The Bahamas was representing the University in the 2017 Miss World Bahamas Beauty Pageant.

You read right!

I was going to compete in Miss Bahamas. Would you just look at God! Won't He Do It!

Not only did He allow me to participate in Miss World Bahamas, but He ensured that I had a sponsor, (something I didn't think about when I was planning to compete.) I had nothing to worry about while competing - everything would be covered by the University.

With a month of downtime after being crowned Miss UB, it was time to get to work. And just like that, I start my prep for the national pageant.

I couldn't wrap my mind around it, but I was competing nationally! It had always been the goal. However, even when I wasn't even looking for or paying attention to it, God made it happen. That just goes to show how good God is. (I'm just saying)

Sometimes it's really up to us to just do the last thing God said to do.

OR

After asking for a thing, believe and know that it is done and on faith, start preparing. After all, success comes when preparation meets opportunity.

I completed my paperwork for the pageant, and it became even more real! But when I attended our boot camp, I got a taste of how real it was about to become. Amusingly, I have no phone during the initial process and showed up on the first day of boot camp with no idea of what to expect and journaled my thoughts during the boot camp.

I wanted to share some of that with you, so I've included a few of those journal entries in this chapter so that you can get a feel of my headspace in May 2017 as Miss University of The Bahamas competing for the title of Miss World Bahamas.

Day 1

It's the first day, and it is pretty interesting. I haven't even gone through half of the day as yet, and boy, there's tension, and I'd even say it's pretty thick. Not to mention GOD decides to be GOD because He is GOD all by himself. He throws me a curveball because He can do that, I guess. I think I know all of the individuals here so far. One of the delegates and I have known each other for 5+ years. My best friends' aunt helped me designed my swimsuit for the Miss Abaco top model competition. What's so funny is that we spoke about entering a pageant together back in 2015. At that time, we had made a pact to break the stereotypes surrounding beauty, and this one cap fits all beauty standards in pageantry. Although after that day, we never spoke about it again. Years later, look at us in the same pageant...ha-ha interesting, I say!

Next, there's another delegate that I'm sure I've crossed paths with before and another I can't put my finger on where I've met her. However, the show must go on, and boy, it's going to be one interesting road to the crown. Two other young ladies arrived, and we all introduce ourselves. Members of the committee step in, and I can already tell it's going to be an interesting weekend.

So many different personalities already, wow!

We went through our first and second sessions of the training. They were inspiring and pushed us to think of issues outside of ourselves.

During our lunch break, I sat and observed all of the interactions going on around me. The saying "you are always being watched" flooded my mind as I looked at the committee members watching each of us. The way we spoke, ate, whether or not we interacted at all and what was being said, "I AM judging you" written all over their faces. So the evening ended on a really good note, in my opinion. We watched the 2016 evening gown preliminary competition with the committee members who are rather TURNT; this can be a good or bad thing depends on how you look at it. But I know that I can't be consumed in the hype of what is and forget why I started in the first place. When I got home, I was exhausted. I laid down, and the next thing I knew, it was about that time to go again.

Day 2

We're off into day two. Everyone gathers together with four contestants here because an early contestant is indeed an early queen, and I wanted to be that. However, the odds weren't in my favor this morning in trying to get here a bit earlier. Today was an interesting day compared to the first day, although we're here for the second time for the same amount of time. Persons began to get more and more relaxed. True colors began to show, and I can surely say mine certainly did. Two other contestants showed up today, totaling 9 contestants that would be vying for this title. All of a sudden, you could feel the intensity. I got lost in my purpose; we had just spoken about this the day before. For some, it was all about the competition. Others, fun; as for me, I can say it was about life change, not just for me but others. See, I've come to understand that it's not about me at all. It's not about what you do and say; it's how you make people feel that matters.

Day 3

No boot camp today. However, as I sit here and reflect on the last two days, I realize that what I am going to do moving forward is implement much-needed prayer time to my life. I think about Abaco and the fact that I wasn't named Miss Abaco 2011 when I competed because it didn't embody what the Lord had for me to represent. It didn't embody who I was. The theme Island Gem, although cute, there was no connection, no real connection. The source didn't necessarily supply the required power needed to continue. I tend to always refer to Abaco, saying so many wonderful things about it because it is indeed my hometown. As Miss University of The Bahamas, I tend to shy away from what that represents. It embodies CHANGE because change is something we tend to run away from. Afraid of what the future holds, what something new might look like, taste like, smell like, be like all because we are content with the way things are, thus no growth and no further enhancement or development of any kind.

So, it has officially begun. I said the same thing at boot camp, but what was shown behind closed doors will be exposed to the public. Interestingly, I did not know what to expect. I felt numb; there were nine contestants but only one queen. I looked around, and all I see is great potential. Hidden talents but this particular journey that I am on, it's just me and GOD...

Challenge accepted.

I know He knows, but there is a disconnect between reality and perception. I am surely walking by faith here. Trusting God and putting it all in his hands. Showing up knowing that He is with me & He knew about this day before I thought about this day. HE STOOD HERE ALREADY.

Well, there you have it, 25-year-old Miss UB. My mindset always intrigued me throughout that entire process. My mind would just go to the furthest of places, then again, I wasn't distracted by a phone, until I got one and welp. What can I say? (Shrug)

Journaling started to dwindle when my district director gave me a phone after boot camp. However, my phone didn't stops me from taking in the full experience. After all, this was my first real taste of the pageant world, I was told. I was able to reflect on the cautions I received and thought to myself, "Well, it couldn't be that bad." And although it wasn't as bad as I'm sure it could have been, it wasn't what I was expecting in some instances. Intriguingly, it wasn't anything crazy either. It was the small and simplest deeds that can throw you for a loop and trip you up. I'm sure you know the saying, "sticks and stones may break our bones," but it doesn't compare to the words that tend to hurt like hell.

It's usually the smallest of things. The straw that broke the camel's back.

I felt like I knew all of the information that the officials provided. I was confident. I felt prepared, and since I was just crowned, there were still some things that I remembered. I was now putting my skills to use as a titleholder and delegate in the national pageant.

I was ready to give 1000 percent. From rehearsal to events and other appearances, I was just going and going! I was thankful that this was all happening during the summer because I couldn't imagine having to do this during school.

I tried my best to stay on top of things. I must admit that I was more proactive and organized in this season of my life. When my officials gave me clothing that was too big, I didn't complain. I humbly said "Thank you!" and went straight to the tailor. When there was something that I needed that wasn't provided, I didn't turn up my nose or act as if I was entitled to it; I just went and got it. I had to always remember that eyes were always on me. No one owed me anything! I had to show up and maintain a standard of excellence… FOR ME!

Break Free Key – *Find solutions rather than focus on the problem. The problem will remain the problem until you solve it, then it's no longer the problem. The sooner you fix it, the sooner you can move on.*

There were moments when I thought this worked in my favor and other instances when I felt like it didn't. I could tell that I wasn't the typical contestant. I would ask certain questions and make suggestions that made someone say to me, "Are you a lawyer?"

And though my response was no, because it was obvious, right?! No?

Their response to me was, "Exactly."

Shrug, not typical.

This idea of not typical followed me throughout the competition. But rather than looking at it as a negative, I thought it was a good thing.

Wow! Growth, because the 'Miss Abaco' me wouldn't have positively received that.

The 'Miss Abaco' me and the me in this pageant were completely different. I was catering to an audience of one! There was no one else there, no one else watching, and I couldn't hear what anyone else had to say, it was just me and God on each stage, down each runway, and at every event.

I loved the space I was in during the competition. When it came down to the finale, the organization huddled us all up in the final hour before the big show. They shared their final words and expectations. Out of everything that was said, one of the things that stuck out to me most was when someone looked me square in the eyes (subconsciously) and said, "there is dignity in defeat."

I immediately started to unpack the statement, "Why defeat; would I lose if I didn't get the crown? Did I not do what I was supposed to do, even when the outcome I was expecting didn't happen; was it a loss?" This statement threw me off completely. Later on, that evening, I got baptized in my Pastor's pool and went to bed to get my beauty sleep to prepare for the big day that was hours away. I had no idea what I was feeling; I was just there, ready to go, and dare I say, I was just chilling until it was time for God to do whatever He had planned. I made it through the on-stage competition, received a few awards during the special presentation segment. It came down to the top 5, and I heard my name. I got on stage, answered my question, and wasn't called back out because I didn't make it past that round. I just knew that I did what I was supposed to do. Some people felt a particular way about the competition, but that night after it was all said and done, I felt GREAT!

I felt full!

I don't think I've ever smiled as big as I did until that night. My support system was all there and there for me. The only thing that I could think of throughout the night was #AudienceOfOne.

I realized now, looking back that God had a plan the entire time, that the answer wasn't "no," but rather it was "not now." He knew that I wasn't ready for what was to come. I can't help but think about the children of Israel when they were coming out of Egypt, and rather than go through the Philistine country, which would have been shorter, God allowed them to take a longer route (Exodus 13:17).

Interestingly, going the long way helped them to stay the course. God knew, according to Exodus, that if they encountered war, hardship, or friction of any sort, they would've changed their minds and went back to the place where they came from. The place I'm referring to is that place of comfort and familiarity.

Think about that and assess whether in instances when it didn't go exactly as planned when it could have been so much easier, is it God leading you the long way?

We often associate winning as the pinnacle of anything we pursue when growth and invaluable lessons can be learned through losing.

So, what did you learn the last time you experienced a loss?

After all, you're never really at a loss if you're learning!

Just because you want it doesn't mean it's needed! God is in the business of giving you what He knows you need rather than giving you what you think you want.

As much as I wanted the title, I wasn't ready for it looking back now. He knew what it was that I needed. He knew that I still needed to grow. He knew my carriage wasn't where it needed to be, and that was far more important to Him because he saw the beginning from the end. Looking back, I can now see how a worldly prize may be appealing for a moment, but the divine perspective and posture last a lifetime.

Put your money where your mouth is and repeat after me!

I am

never

defeated.

I am

only

Uncaged.

AUTHENTIC TRUTH

The day after the competition, I needed ice cream, and I guess all of the emotions surrounding the final night settled in.

Let's just say that I didn't exactly feel like how I felt when I left the convention center that night. After the adrenaline and sugar wore off, I couldn't help but question what happened.

It had nothing to do with the pageant per-say but more to do with what God said, which didn't add up... quite frankly, I was a bit disappointed.

I had so many questions that I felt needed answers.

For starters, "What's really up, God? I mean, you said all of these things, yet it's not happening. What changed? Why didn't it happen? Was I not "anointed" anymore? Did it mean that I would no longer receive the promise?" I was happy that night because this sense of peace came over me, but when the dust settled, so to speak, the feeling in my gut wasn't exactly settling.

A lot of what I was feeling was me trying to understand what I did wrong, not to change the outcome or anything but simple to understand.

I had, well, kind of still have (it's a work in progress) this thing where I need to know everything! The who, what, when, where, and why: I was struggling because I didn't have the answers to any of these questions. Not having the answers and not knowing left tons of room for me to start questioning myself and my abilities in a time when I knew that God had a plan. Duh, I knew that all things work together for good, but it didn't change the fact that it didn't feel good.

This is where faith comes in because even though I didn't feel like it, nor was I seeing what I thought I would be, I still reminded myself of the promises of God because He couldn't lie.

PERIOD!

When God spoke, I listened, and I stood on that.

> **Break Free Key** - *Find your anchor, that thing that you need to always go back to when you start to feel like it's not adding up. Find something to get you back to the place where you need to be because your feelings can easily lead you to somewhere you think you want to be just because it feels good. And it won't always feel good but stay planted until it's time for you to break up out of the ground.*

The circumstances didn't look like what I thought they would. I still believed because the GOD that I serve (my anchor) is much bigger, like exceedingly abundantly above kind of bigger. (Ephesians 3:20) What made this situation even more interesting was during my quiet time one day, I heard God say, "plot twist," and instantly, a million thoughts started running through my mind regarding what He said.

"What does that even mean? Was there another crown? Another pageant?"

I left the room I was in to go and share my thoughts with my second mom. As soon as I walked into the living room, out of nowhere, she says "You should do another pageant." I smiled as I thought about what had just come to mind moments ago. Later that week, and as I'm leaving church, a former personal trainer asks me to join the same pageant my second mom had mentioned.

I suddenly start to think of all of the instances where someone said my title wrong because it was too long, confusing, or complicated to say. Instead of addressing me as "Miss University of The Bahamas," I was often referred to as "Miss Universe Bahamas."

Hmm.

Maybe God was on to something here.

Why didn't He just have me compete in that pageant in the first place? As I try to enjoy what's left of my summer, two weeks to be exact, I couldn't seem to shake the thought of competing again. The desire grew stronger and stronger. However, I still had a reign to complete, and my work wasn't done just yet. I pulled myself together to continue to work on my platform and figure out my space.

There was no more stage, no camera, no lights, no social media challenges, no following, just the girl on her journey of truth.

I liked that girl, and I wanted to continue to be her after all. Even though the crown was a goal, it wasn't the only goal. More importantly, I understood that it wasn't the crown that would make the girl rather the girl that would ultimately make the crown.

So, I went on to complete my reign, wanting to ensure I left an undeniable legacy. After it was all said and done, I went on to continue my quest to be uncaged. The pursuit of showing that I, in my own right, broke out of the cage set before me by myself and others to be the queen I was meant to be. From the moment we are were born, there's a crown on our heads. Just because it isn't visible doesn't mean it isn't there, nor does it diminish or take away from the light that we carry.

Yes, you! You carry light to brighten the world of those you come in contact with and to shed light to those dark places you've experienced too. Some ten years later, with all of the hurt and pain I felt in the dark, I can see them clearly because I tapped into my light. It's time you tap into yours.

Life beyond the crown for me would now transition from a physical crown to the invisible one that I always had. Having the same confidence in the invisible crown that I did with the physical. Making the best out of the crown that I did have instead of being hung up on the one I didn't. After all, there is only one true crown, which is ultimately the only crown that will last in the end.

Put your money where your mouth is and repeat after me!

His will

for my life

is more

important

than

a win

in life.

BONUS: FAREWELL SPEECH

Miss University of The Bahamas 2017
Farewell Speech

The crown, the sash, and the steps of Miss University of The Bahamas represent more than an institution; it represents the dreams and aspirations of what tertiary education embodies for every single Bahamian across the length and breadth of our archipelago. As the first Miss University of The Bahamas, this thought was the charter for my year; my experiences were not only for Nyisha, the girl from Abaco but for the entire Bahamas. I knew from the moment that I entered the pageant that it was about dreaming and dreaming big, a dream that gives birth to change, and one that would provide hope. A tale to recite to young people, all people that it's never too late; if I can do it, so can you.

As I turn the pages in this chapter of my life, I pause to bow to the Almighty God, who is my King of Kings, my Savior, the Author of this incredible faith that is inside of me. Thank you, Abba, for writing your story on my heart.

To Joe Stubbs and Traven Cargill: without you, there would be no Miss University of The

Bahamas. You have been both amazing to me. You have allowed me to be the Queen you knew I could be without judgment, criticism, or unnecessary limitations. You have allowed me to reign in my truth. I thank you and the entire Miss UB Committee for your unfailing faith and your support of the dream.

To the University of The Bahamas, you are the breeding ground of greatness and expectancy. You have carved your space in my heart.

To my mothers, Nitta and Fany, you are the bones of my spine; your steady voices keeping me straight and true. You have both taught me that it's not about the life you speak but the life you live that truly matters. It is the life that you both have lived that taught me that fairy tales are more than true; that it is not because dragons exist, but because dragons can be beaten. I love you. I am the woman I am because you both exist in my life.

To Aaron, thank you for walking on this journey with me. For all you do, for who you are, and the way you believe in me. I love you, and I am forever grateful that you're in my life.

Undeniably, it took a village, a University, a Nation, my family, friends, and supporters who continue to motivate and shape me. You all demand the high standards of Miss University of The Bahamas, a Standard Bearer to lift high the ideals and philosophies of our great Bahama land.

To the 2018 Contestants, you have taken a step of a thousand miles. Continue to wear the crown you were born with. You are a Queen! Know that it is in the process that you are refined. You are all diamonds, strong and sturdy women who will represent this Institution and this Nation with pride.

As I remove this crown from my head tonight, I will remember the strong blue hues. Blue is the color of the sky and sea. It is often associated with depth and stability. It symbolizes trust, loyalty, wisdom, confidence, intelligence, faith, truth, and heaven. It is considered beneficial to the mind and body. I entrust this legacy to the young lady who will be crowned Miss UB; embrace your journey. We are here to support you every step of the way. Take your candle, go light your world.

Ubuntu! I am because we are!

ACKNOWLEDGMENT

This book would not be possible if it were not for GOD. I've never felt qualified to write a book; however, I'm grateful to have a God that doesn't call the qualified but qualifies those whom He calls.

To my family and friends, I always strived to show you all that the world is at your feet. Thank you for pushing and fueling me to show you what the world has to offer.

To my former pageant directors, coaches, mentors, & sisters, thank you for not just inspiring me but also inspiring and challenging other young ladies out there.

CONNECT WITH ME

Website: **www.nyishatilus.com**

Social Media: **@IAmNyishaTilus**

Made in the USA
Monee, IL
31 May 2021